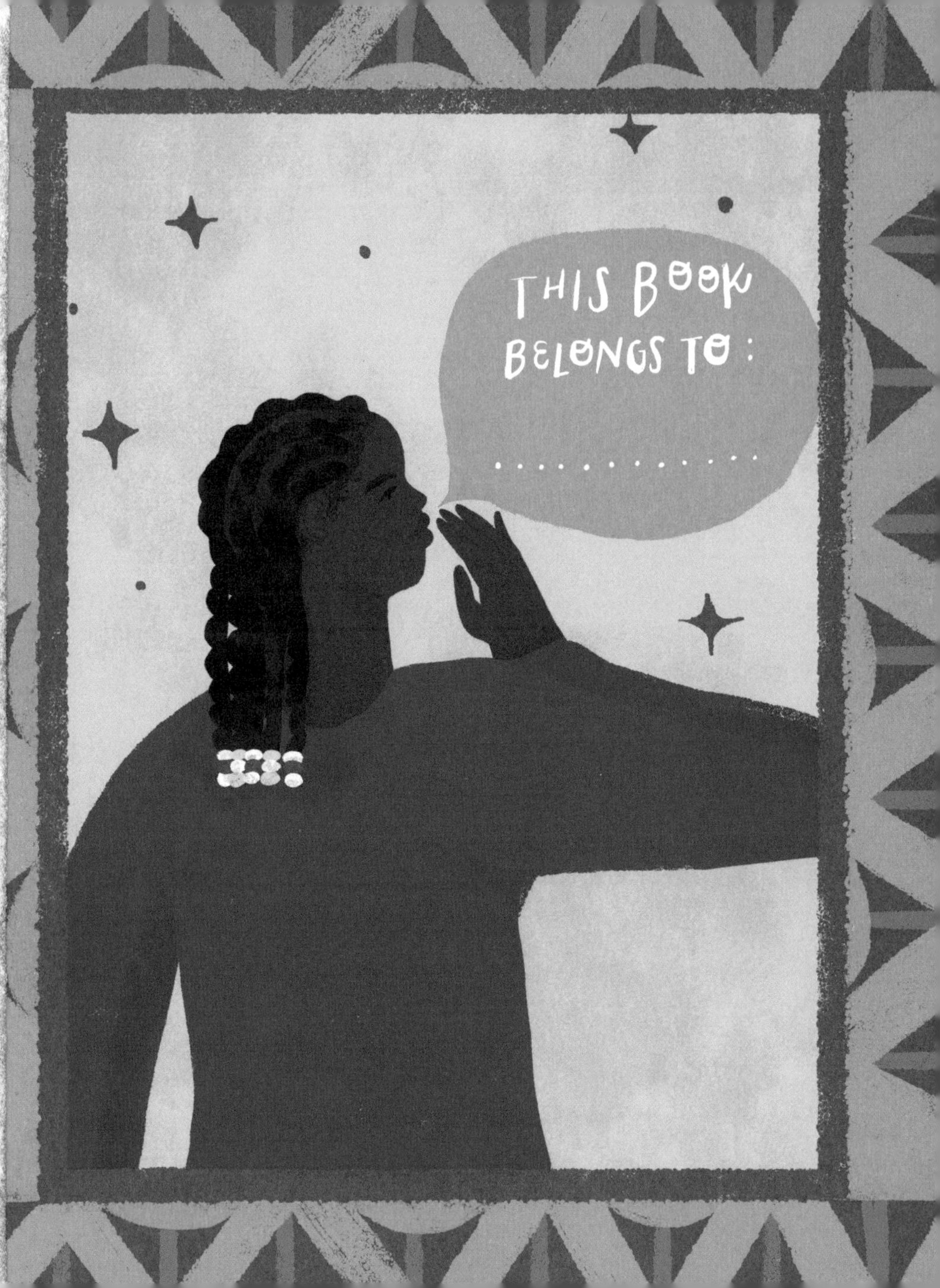
THIS BOOK
BELONGS TO :
. . . .

HER

NAME

Zetta Elliott

ILLUSTRATED BY *Loveis Wise*

DISNEP · JUMP AT THE SUN

LOS ANGELES   NEW YORK

First Edition, January 2020
10 9 8 7 6 5 4 3 2 1
FAC-034274-19333
Printed in the United States of America

Copyright credits for permissions are located on page 83.

This book is set in Bulmer MT Pro/Monotype.
Designed by Mary Claire Cruz and Maria Fernandez

Library of Congress Cataloging-in-Publication Data

Names: Elliott, Zetta, author. • Wise, Loveis, illustrator.
Title: Say her name / by Zetta Elliott ; illustrated by Loveis Wise.
Description: First hardcover edition. • New York : Jump at the Sun, 2020.
Identifiers: LCCN 2019002971 • ISBN 9781368045247 (paper over board)
Subjects: LCSH: Young adult poetry, American.
Classification: LCC PS3605.L463 A6 2020 • DDC 811/.6—dc23
LC record available at https:// lccn.loc.gov/2019002971

Visit www.Disneybooks.com

for us
Z.E.

CONTENTS

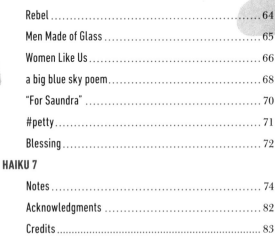

INTRODUCTION

I sometimes write poetry, but I am not a poet. At least, I've never thought of myself that way. I'm a writer of plays, novels, essays, and books for children. If I got stuck while working on a story, I might stop and write a half dozen haiku. But on average, I used to write just one poem a year—and only when I was angry.

Then at the start of 2018, Paquita Campoverde at the Brooklyn Public Library asked me to prepare high school students for a tribute to Pulitzer Prize-winning poet Gwendolyn Brooks. Years before, I'd done a similar event for beloved children's poet Shel Silverstein, and "I Make Magic" was one of the poems I wrote as an example for my second-grade students.

When I discovered my teen writers weren't familiar with Brooks and her contemporaries, I began introducing poetry by other Black women. I shared my "mentor texts"—poems I have admired, studied, and taught for years. These poets helped me to find my own voice and I hoped they would inspire my students, too.

We only had three sessions together in January, but I encouraged my teens to continue writing. I did the same, and by the end of March, two poems inspired by Brooks's "We Real Cool" had blossomed into forty poems about the vulnerability, strength, and magic of Black women and girls.

It wasn't hard to find inspiration. Every day I saw examples of Black excellence reported online alongside accounts of appalling brutality. I still wrote when I was angry, but the core of rage is pain, which means I turned to poetry because I was hurting.

The past few years have been difficult for many of us, and writing has certainly helped me cope with what often feels like an endless stream of bad news. Still, some days are better than others when it comes to managing my emotions. I've lived with depression and anxiety since I was a teenager, and finding a healthy balance between hope and fear is a daily struggle. In poems like "self/care" and "appetite" I have tried to be honest—and compassionate— about my own limitations.

In my twenties I wrote a dissertation on the lynching of Black women; I was braver then, more willing to draw close to the things that frightened me. Now that I am middle-aged, I find I'm more inclined to step back than to rush ahead. I still believe, however, that we do not have the right to look away. And when you are a witness, you have a duty to testify. My research on lynching taught me that power goes to those who are best able to represent their victimization—no easy task for Black women and girls who are rarely, if ever, read as innocent in this society. But as Zora Neale Hurston famously warned, "If you are silent about your pain, they'll kill you and say you enjoyed it."

This book is my way of bearing witness. I have not lost a loved one to police violence, but I have been changed by seeing my sisters and brothers shamed, shot, and slammed to the ground. In response I have not marched—my protest exists mostly on the page. Sometimes it feels like that's not enough; other times I recognize that we each have a role to play. In "How to Resist" I tried to express the range of protest possibilities, ending with the most radical act of all: *feel something.*

I am grateful for the survivors, scholars, students, and activists whose daring and determination place them in the streets or in the courts, in the thick of protests on campus or online. Despite the risk, they are out in front, inspiring us with their courage; they are the leaders we need right now.

The title of this collection comes from the campaign launched by the African American Policy Forum in 2014. I wish it was automatic—that violence against Black women, girls, and femmes received the same media attention and community outrage. I wish more Black men and boys spoke out, stood up, and marched for us the way we grieve, rage, and mobilize on their behalf. But I am heartened by the way Black women have founded organizations and movements to insist that *all* Black Lives Matter.

I am equally grateful for the artists whose work helps us to envision a better future. Four of my mentor poems are included in this collection, and I hope readers will hear in my poems the "echo" of Lucille Clifton, Nikki Giovanni, Audre Lorde, and Phillis Wheatley. I have deliberately "sampled" some of their verses in order to place my poems in conversation with the poet-elders who showed me what was possible.

In 1977 the Combahee River Collective published a powerful, provocative statement. It, too, has been a mentor text for me; I can recite some parts by heart, and I revisit their manifesto when I find myself in need of inspiration. "We realize that the only people who care enough about us to work consistently for our liberation are us." We do have allies, but some days it feels like all we have is each other. This book of poetry is for us. I love us.

—ZE, 12/28/18

take your sister's hand
twine your fingers between hers
face the world as one

young, gifted, and Black
willing to sacrifice all
to see justice done

I woke up like this
fierce, focused, and ready to
fight for my people

BLACK GIRL MIRACLE

Black girl
you are more
than magic
you are a miracle
because we were never
meant to survive
not as human beings
yet despite their best efforts
to grind us down
still we rise
we strut
dazzle
& defy the odds
to claim the gold
solve the equation
hoist the trophy
break all barriers
& set every trend
so let them shun us
we won't dim our shine
we will luxuriate in the beauty
we see in each other
we will protect ourselves

with rituals of healing
we will dance beneath the new moon
and pray beside the sea
so that the ancestors know
their blessings
have been
received

LULLABY

beloved

let me sing you a lullaby

let me wrap you in a tender embrace

and rock you till you sleep

let my flesh shield yours

from bigots' bullets

clinical indifference

academic aggression

and the callous gaze that

sees a monster lurking inside

your hooded eyes

let me school you

fill your mind with magic

myths and truths

no bars could contain

let me build a world

where you are safe to play

in the park

and swim

in the pool

and sit

at your desk

and sleep
in your house
and laugh
in the street
so that when you
walk home from the store
you reach me
alive

BLACK LIVES MATTER

for Alicia, Opal & Patrisse

like alchemists
you took our shame
and turned it into pride
you made rage respectable again
and showed us how to move
our bodies as one to occupy
the streets where we are slain

beloved trinity
we heeded your call
and followed your lead
got ourselves in formation
got ourselves to the polls
to the precincts
and all the places we've never been
wanted or seen or heard

they will try to pass the mic
to the brothers standing behind you
but we know the burden you bear
as women Black immigrant queer
we will not let them erase you

you are visible and valuable to us
we humbly thank you, sisters
for coining this affirmation
for sparking this revolution
for building this vital movement
for upholding us with this steady love

HOW TO RESIST

march
curse
fume
cry
but save some of your salt
to cure the rage so
it lasts even longer

write a poem
write a check

take a social media break
take a long bath
put lotion on your body
then put your body in the street

don't waste your words on frauds
be strategically silent
or find the spaces of denial
and shatter the silence
with your screams

close your ears to the lies
but listen to the cries
of the weak and wounded
keep the truth deep inside
safe from the filthy fingers
that warp everything they touch

let it throb
ache
and break
over and over again but
don't harden your heart
harden your resolve instead

most of all

feel something
feel something
feel something

DON'T TOUCH MY HAIR

don't touch my hair
these locks
are worth
more than gold
my crowning glory
is my personal wealth
so keep your hands
to yourself
I have no time
for your
simple curiosity
or bald contempt
(do you wash it? comb it?
it looks so unkempt!)
you can
ban my braids
try to tame
my 'fro
even snatch
my wig
but you can
never displace
the ancient roots

that reach deep
into my soul
and bind me to
the very first Mother
Africa springs proud
and defiant from
my oiled scalp
my coils curls
and kinks
will persist
so I insist
that respect be
shown
my halo
is not yours
to regulate

SELF/CARE

some days
it's okay
to eat cupcakes
instead
of kale
to pull on
stretchy pants
and a hoodie
curl up on the
sofa and watch
online videos
of baby goats
prancing in
pajamas
it's okay to
curl into your
pillow when
there's no one
else to hold
and let your tears
soak the foam
then order
a large three

topping pizza
and finish that pint
of coffee toffee
bar crunch
without anybody's
help

other days
you can go for
a long run
hit the gym
or walk
in the park
find a body
of water
breathe deep
lungfuls of fresh air
see a matinee
by yourself
put on your
cute clothes
take a selfie
have a salad
with your slice

doodle in
your journal
pet a dog
you don't own
see the beauty
in small things
see the beauty
in yourself
even as you
don your armor
to make it through
another day

PANTHER

*for the women of Wakanda and
the sisters in Oakland*

if you want to be a princess
that's your prerogative
(be like Shuri; learn to code)
I would rather be
a panther
sleek and wild
an untamable beast
who already knows
how it feels to be free
a fierce fighter
feared and endangered
protective of her young
and ready to defend
her territory
you don't have to rock
dark glasses
black leather
and a perfect Afro

wear a dashiki
if you want
just keep their
legacy alive

feed the poor
heal the sick
fight the power
know your rights
and teach the youth
the truth

driving while Black and
woman can get you killed so
check your blind spot, girl

rage is a blade so
hold it carefully, keep it
close but safely sheathed

just like Fannie Lou
I question America
who will answer me

FOR MY PEOPLE

if you ever dream
of mothering dragons
if you take tea with hobbits
or call Hermione kin
if you aren't afraid
to walk leopards on leashes
or ride on alligators
don't lose your nerve
folks may stare in wonder
be quick to mock & malign
but deep down they marvel at your daring
& envy your courage to be open
about what it is you truly love
it's not easy being alien
but know that you are not alone
we are abandoning the margins
rejecting the boundaries of Blackness
& making more room
for everyone

WE SHALL OVERCOME

don't let
the beauty
of this world
lose its allure

remember
even roses
can
climb
walls

we have
been designed
to overcome

SONNET FOR IDA

If I could wrap my people in my arms,
I'd take them far from this chaotic place
and shield my kin from every type of harm
so that despair no longer shades each face.
But conductors always understood not
all slaves can see the chains they wear, and roots
so deeply bound to hostile soil cannot
bear to be exposed—even in pursuit
of freedom. Ida tried to lead us west
but no land keeps its promise. The needle
spins around and round, the compass useless
in my palm. How can I serve my people?
Perhaps my arms should never seek to bind
a race destined to redeem humankind.

"A WOMAN SPEAKS"
BY AUDRE LORDE

Moon marked and touched by sun
my magic is unwritten
but when the sea turns back
it will leave my shape behind.
I seek no favor
untouched by blood
unrelenting as the curse of love
permanent as my errors
or my pride
I do not mix
love with pity
nor hate with scorn
and if you would know me
look into the entrails of Uranus
where the restless oceans pound.

I do not dwell
within my birth nor my divinities
who am ageless and half-grown
and still seeking
my sisters
witches in Dahomey
wear me inside their coiled cloths
as our mother did
mourning.

I have been woman
for a long time
beware my smile
I am treacherous with old magic
and the noon's new fury
with all your wide futures
promised
I am
woman
and not white.

ZETTA ELLIOTT

MERMAIDS

I am still seeking my sisters
swallowed by dense forests
and insatiable seas
the trees guided some girls
back to their homes but
the waves simply
took their tears
with silent sympathy

now bodies litter the beach
flesh turned to flotsam
this is no fairy tale
though the story is grim

I once thought
pirates only smuggled
the most precious things
black gold
they called us

still they emptied the *Zong*
and sent 133 souls
to the bottom of the sea

sisters you are not refuse
though nations refuse you entry
until your bloated bodies
bob atop their waves
your lives matter
perhaps if we link arms
across the sea we can
stop this traffic too

till then may your
souls find peace with
the mother of the sea
may our kin who leapt
laughing into the
yawning jaws of sharks
wreathe you with pearls
and may you tread
weightless upon the seabed
as the ancestors
guide you back home

TSUNAMI

we will kneel
on the field &
we will climb
up that flagpole &
we will tear down   we will accept your disappointment
that monument &   the shame is not ours
we will march   we will exceed your expectations
through the streets &   you never saw our true potential
we will occupy   we will not apologize for our rage
your sacred spaces &   you earned every drop
we will disrupt
traffic, making
you LATE &
we will shout
down new Nazis
spewing the same old
message of hate

WE MATTER

BLM

OUR LIVES MATTER!

a tsunami
is coming
we are sounding
the alarm

APPETITE

sometimes I eat my rage

sometimes it eats me

how do I protest?
my words march across the page
defiantly Black

queenhood divides us
when one woman is placed
above all others

we all need sisters
like Solange who will fiercely
fight on our behalf

I MAKE MAGIC

some look for
the shimmer of fairy
dust on rose petals
some wish on
a shooting star
some mix up a potion
or utter a spell
some follow the
rainbow to
its pot of gold
but I
make magic
with the words
in my mind
I weave syllables
into silver
I tell
lyrical lies
that illuminate
the darkest mind
and make
all doubters
BELIEVE

WE ARE WISE

We are wise. We
will rise. We

fight hate. We
tempt fate. We

risk all. We
stand tall. We

provoke. We
stay woke.

WE CAN'T BREATHE

We can't breathe. We
still seethe. We

stay mad. We
break bad. We

hold rage. We
rampage. We

scare you. We
scared too.

THE SOURCE

No one at school knows what happens at the pier and Kevonn plans to keep it that way. I don't blame him. And I won't tell. On this side of the bridge he's got a home, parents who love him, homeboys who show him respect on and off the court. He's got what so many of us have had taken away, but it comes at a price. Here there is no magic, no glamour. No feathery lashes, skin dusted with gold. Bodies bold and free. To touch, strut, twirl—just BE. Here there is still risk, but nowhere near the same reward. So he keeps his head down, looks no one in the eye. Laughs at every corny joke, gives as good as he gets. Today in Bio I watched as he whistled on cue when Keisha walked by, switching that perfect ass. Tyrell puckered his lips but she gave him the finger, eyes rolling as her diamond-tipped talon caught the light. His boys howled so Tyrell had to save face: "Keep steppin', bitch. I don't want nothin' black but a Xbox." Then Ms. G turned from the board, looked him straight in the eye. "Boy," she demanded, "who taught you to hate your source?"

SACRED

Do you not know that your body is a temple
of the Holy Spirit within you, which you have from God?
You are not your own, Mama reminds me
You are our pearl, Pastor says from the pulpit
I am a good girl, Mama's consolation
for one son in Rikers and another on the street
one night out couldn't hurt, I tell myself
one night with my friends instead of my books
one drink just to help me relax
and the room starts spinning
it's easier to go down stairs than up
so I go to the basement
find a sofa to lie on
wake to one hand pushing up my skirt
two others clamped around my wrists
a fourth on my ankle and a
heavy palm on the back of my head
pressing my screams into the cushion
Do you not know that my body is a temple
after a while I stop counting stop screaming
the hands let go since there is
no fight left in my limbs
tears soak the cushion

their laughter scrapes my ears
then eternity ends and they are gone
I slide onto the shag carpet
pull myself up the wall
my body is screaming
but I stagger through the dark room
to the door promised by a draft of cold air
make my way up the block shivering vomiting
gripping fence rails and lampposts
feeling the disdain of neighbors who once
beamed at me with pride
Do you know *why*
I want to ask them
How can it be that
my body this temple
has been defiled?

MIC CHECK

mic check
one two
one two
Is this thing on?
Can you hear me now?
Gimme a beat—no
wait

If my words don't rhyme
will you still take the time
to listen and learn
or must I earn
your attention
with lyrical pretension?

My words bloom on the page;
you won't find me onstage
sculpting air with my hands
as my voice expands
to fill the darkness . . .

There's more than one way
to be a poet.

Poems ring in my ears
like bells no one else hears
they grow quietly
like moss on stone
penned in secrecy
once I'm alone

This antisocial introvert
is tender-hearted and easily hurt
but I turn the pain into verses
so free the poem nurses
me back to health.

I can't rank emcees,
and won't try to appease
the poetry police.
My words are plain,
my message direct.
If you find me mundane,
just try to respect
my delivery:
unique—like me.

SAY HER NAME

Say her name and solemnly vow
Never to forget, nor allow
Our sisters' lives to be erased;
Their presence cannot be replaced.
This senseless slaughter must stop now.

We toiled in fields with sack and plow,
Swung next to our men on the bough.
Were violated, called unchaste.
Say her name.

Some say to Black men we must bow;
Our rights will trickle down somehow.
No problem's solved until it's faced,
But we have no time left to waste.
Our daughters with strength we endow—
Say her name.

you fear the shadow
but it is the substance of
us you most desire

your smile is not owed
to any man—genuine
compliments are free

magical Black girls
are made of starshine and clay
gaze at us in awe

"WON'T YOU CELEBRATE WITH ME"

BY LUCILLE CLIFTON

won't you celebrate with me
what i have shaped into
a kind of life? i had no model.
born in babylon
both nonwhite and woman
what did i see to be except myself?
i made it up
here on this bridge between
starshine and clay,
my one hand holding tight
my other hand; come celebrate
with me that everyday
something has tried to kill me
and has failed.

TO BE FREE

I wish I knew how it feels to be free.
Is it roots or chains that keep us earthbound?
Maybe the stars do hold our destiny.

Displaced person, unwelcome refugee,
Alien, banned, forced to live underground . . .
I wish I knew how it feels to be free.

We cross deserts seeking sanctuary,
Then the sea swallows us without a sound;
Maybe the stars do hold our destiny.

If we cannot live here with dignity,
A better home must finally be found
So we may know how it feels to be free.

Our true source is a distant galaxy;
The journey here, a mystery profound.
The stars hold the key to our destiny.

Yearning for home binds our community;
Across the planet our cries will resound:
We want to know how it feels to be free!
To dwell amidst stars is our destiny.

HER CLOUD

in math class
she spits rhymes
pencil drumming on the desk
I sit one row back
pretending to solve
equations scribbled
on the board
but really I'm
writing down her
dope lyrics as
she says them
over and over
committing them to memory
she doesn't know that
I am her cloud
she doesn't see
how I hover
try to shield her
from the glare
of sons
she doesn't care
what people think
I wish I could be

in/different
like her
but for now it's enough
just to sit here behind her
maybe one day she'll
realize I've got her
back

THE CROWN

if you love me
abdicate
forfeit the crown they
would place upon your head
let humility bend your neck instead
remember when you stand in the pulpit
that to minister is to serve
see in me your own divinity
raise your fist
smash pedestals
be gentle with yourself
take my hand
walk beside me and I will show you
how to create a world within yourself

try a little tenderness
because my heart is full of love
for you, for us, and for all our people
you don't have to be the man
we can fight the man together
if you're content to
be levelly human
remain humane
fight for my right
to be free
like I fight for
yours

ANANSI

sister
trickster
snare me with
your sticky strands
wrap me in silver silk &
teach me how to ~~deceive~~
sow doubt as I weave a
web of wily tales that
will lure those who
listen closer to
my truth

RUNAWAY

in a starlit swamp

with hounds baying behind me

I focus on the soles of your feet

flashing like mirrors in the dark

no map to guide me

just your sweat-soaked back

I could shut my eyes and track you by scent

this train we have formed will never stop

should you stagger and fall

I will be there to raise you up

we will reach the river together

because there is no

freedom for me

without

you

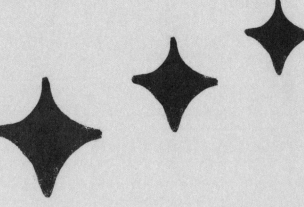

"ON BEING BROUGHT FROM AFRICA TO AMERICA"

BY PHILLIS WHEATLEY

'Twas mercy brought me from my *Pagan* land,
Taught my benighted soul to understand
That there's a God, that there's a *Saviour* too:
Once I redemption neither sought nor knew.
Some view our sable race with scornful eye,
"Their colour is a diabolic die."
Remember, *Christians*, *Negros*, black as *Cain*,
May be refin'd, and join th' angelic train.

ON BEING BUILDERS OF A NEW WORLD

A riot's the language of the unheard
Our race, besieged, has had its dreams deferred.
Africa lives on, in blood, root, and bone;
Yet when we are murdered, our names aren't known.
We cannot breathe, in obscurity die,
Yet march with outrage *we* have been denied.
Remember, *Brothers*, Sisters' lives count, too;
As equals we could build this world anew.

dreams sustain us so
feed your imagination
and reshape the world

stolen bodies on
stolen land; our people know
that water is life

when the sea turns back
the souls left behind will rise
to shame the new world

ASCENSION

for Sabriya

things
that are buried
can still rise

seeds sleep through
these bleak winter months
but flourish in the spring
when sunlight summons them
from the soil

spirits rise
too

so know
sweet sister
that the solstice is here
days will grow longer
and sunrays will soon
warm the earth

so shift the shroud of
dead leaves from your limbs
let air wash like fuel
over your pierced flesh
then rise like an
avenging angel
like Christ
anarchist

spread your wings
of flame phoenix
and burn so bright
that your immolation
cleanses us all

join the others
as they streak
the black sky silver
showering traitors and
disciples alike with the
dust of distant stars

at the window
I will bear witness
beside my twinkling tree
softly singing
pie Jesu
dona eis requiem

FREE THEM ALL

free Bresha

free Rousse

free Ahed

free Cyntoia

free _____

free _____

free _____

free all political prisoners

free your mind

break the bars

stretch your heart

dream a radical future

become an abolitionist

SISTER

you are the mirror
that never betrays me
you are the balm
that heals all my wounds
when the fight leaves me weary
you take up my sword & shield
when storms leave me battered
it's with you I find refuge
you are the peace
of companionable silence
you are the riot
of unrestrained laughter
you are the sun and the shadow
ahead, above, and behind me

sister
you are the bond
never forfeited
the promise
always kept
you are the blessing
that compensates for
the world's injustice

ZETTA ELLIOTT

we are bound
not by blood but by choice
love alone makes us kin
your eyes always see my whole self
who I am, have been, and could yet become
you are my most trusted witness
and when I fail, your compassion
teaches me to forgive myself

our paths may diverge
sister
but loyalty will keep us close
in an inconstant world
full of virtual friends
devotion is a gift
and for that
I thank you

HANDS UP

up

hands

don't shoot

up

rise

don't stop

up

head

don't despair

don't surrender

don't let go

of your dreams

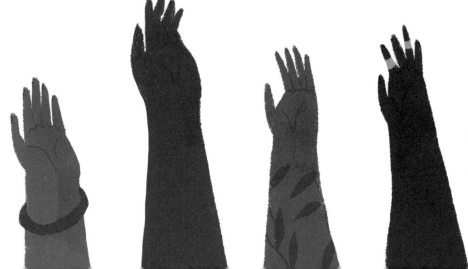

MOUSE

niggas aint shit
some of em at least
I should know
been in these streets
long enough
not sayin Im perfect
but a no from a female
aint never set me off
plenty fish in the sea

Mama say
why you callin my child
a rodent
it aint like that I say
rats is nasty
but a mouse
just a little bitty
critter lookin for
a safe place to live
in this big old world

my Mouse
she too little to strap a real blade

so I got her a knife just her size
no bigger than a pen
werent bout the blade
it was bout makin her feel like
she could always fight back
in case any nigga stepped to her like that

friday nights Mouse be out with her friends
they go over to the Village
not cruisin or nothin
just seein and bein seen
I aint worried cause I know
she in good hands
shit Fee and Lina bigger 'n
tougher than some dudes I know
but some fool got his feelins hurt
when he found out he was
knockin on the wrong door
Fee got in his face
told him to step
but he grabbed Nubia
ripped the gold locks from her head
my little mouse

she aint nothin if not loyal
took one look at the blood
drippin from her friends scalp
pulled out her knife and jabbed him
just like I taught her
then another brotha shows up
sees this punk swingin on sistas
says, fight me, bitch
but its Mouse doin a bid
cause the papers called her and Fee
and Lina and Nu a pack of wolves
when all they done
is look out for each other

prisons too big a place for my baby sista
if I could Id do the time for her
its my fault anyway
I just wanted Mouse to be safe
cause these streets aint no joke
I learned how to handle myself but
they still took me out in the end

now Im just
a face on a mural
a breath with no words
my apology just enough
to flutter the flame
of the candles
mama lights
and leaves
by the
wall

GET UP

get up

        (get on up)

get up

        (get on up)

don't stay on the scene

remember Nina said
you've got to learn
to leave the table
when love's no
longer being
served

inherent value

means you were born precious and

owe no one service

no wall can contain

ancestral aspirations

our lives, their victory

in your DNA

live your foremothers' best traits

display them with pride

REBEL

I rebel because
I am not a good negress
uppity and proud
I've forgotten my place and
don't need you to remind me

MEN MADE OF GLASS

men made of glass
beware my smile
with lips closed
I can cast a spell
that will reduce you to shards

I draw magic from a well
more ancient than you can fathom
I commune with unsettled spirits
listening to their lament

you spilled my sisters' blood
because they denied you
shame led to slaughter
indefensible panic

my sisters are black pearls
far beyond your valuation
you were never worthy
and now your time is up

WOMEN LIKE US

Grandma couldn't kiss me and all her meals went through the blender because of the drug that once ran through her veins. Her kisses, puckerless and wet, were pressed with force but filled with love. Grandma couldn't kiss or chew, but her stories didn't cease. She passed on what she wanted preserved—tales told deliberately and arranged like the orderly jars of pulpy tomatoes she canned for future consumption.

Her brokenness embarrassed her but I hope she knew she was not to blame, that the darkness living inside of her was a curse *and* a blessing—an insistent invitation to seek refuge, to withdraw and find relief from pain's blinding glare.

I wish I had known at sixteen that I wasn't the first in our family to slide into the abyss. Over time I learned how to find my way out, buoyed by borrowed hope and the same frantic energy that wrung my grandmother's gnarled hands. In the abyss I find respite from the everyday hustle that grinds me down. I grind my teeth down with worry but when the darkness envelops me, I sleep with total surrender. When I wake, anxiety insists I get up and record my dreams. This is my uneasy balance.

There were some stories Grandma kept to herself. Years after her death, I learned my grandmother was a survivor. I hope it wasn't shame that censored her. I hope she knew I wouldn't have loved her less.

They say the dead never die so long as we speak their names; I proudly bear hers. I hope my grandmother knows that I am not ashamed of this inheritance. I know what it cost a woman in her position to ask for help. She wanted to live with less pain. She charged me with telling our story.

Women like us may be wounded, but we can also heal. Women like us are not disposable. Women like us must testify.

A BIG BLUE SKY POEM

a sparrow

pecks at crumbs in a Brooklyn gutter

builds a nest from the scraps of others' lives

she teaches her young how to forage

so they too can soar into the big blue sky

the tree

that is their home was once

a seed small as its chance of survival

yet now that oak towers above us

its roots strong enough to rupture concrete

in desperate times

search the city for signs of survival

remember that we all live

beneath the same big blue sky

that stretches unbroken over borders

walls

seas

all the things that divide us

beyond earth's dome
sky blue deepens to infinite blackness
stars swirl & burn in boundless galaxies
that is the source to which we will return
for we are made of starshine & clay

when Sojourner's mam
wept for her stolen children
she looked up at the stars
and through the veil of her tears
knew that starlight shone upon them too

so love
when you find yourself
raging beneath the big blue sky
know that you are not alone
when night falls we will stand
each in our corner of the world
and find solace in the same bright stars

"FOR SAUNDRA"

BY NIKKI GIOVANNI

i wanted to write
a poem
that rhymes
but revolution doesn't lend
itself to be-bopping

then my neighbor
who thinks i hate
asked—do you ever write
tree poems—i like trees
so i thought
i'll write a beautiful green tree poem
peeked from my window
to check the image
noticed that the school yard was covered
with asphalt

no green—no trees grow
in manhattan

then, well, i thought the sky
i'll do a big blue sky poem
but all the clouds have winged
low since no-Dick was elected

so i thought again
and it occurred to me
maybe i shouldn't write
at all
but clean my gun
and check my kerosene supply

perhaps these are not poetic
times
at all

#PETTY

if cut-eye could kill
I'd be dead by now
but popularity has never
been my priority
so turn your back
or walk on by
I'm not numb
to sneers and snubs
but I can't do more than
own my mistakes
and my privilege
I won't apologize
for existing
or using my voice
to speak my truth
talk about my mother
if it means that much to you
I have work to do
you can tell me to
stay in my lane
but it's not a race
I will follow my own path
at my own pace

and let you do the same
may God grant
traveling mercies
to us all

BLESSING

May you have a resilient spirit,
and a compassionate heart,
the desire to heal,
and the will to forgive.
May you never exhaust
your capacity for kindness.
May you always find peace
in your home and in your mind.

May your eyes be awake
to the beauty all around you.
May your ears be tuned
to the varied songs of life.
May your arms always be ready
to embrace those needing comfort,
and may even the simplest blessings
fill your heart with gratitude.

indictments are rare
like snow in the Sahara
or cops behind bars

innocence belongs
to other people's children
ours are born condemned

stop killing us stop
killing us stop killing us
stop killing us STOP

NOTES

"Black Girl Miracle"

This poem draws upon the work of several Black feminists. I borrowed the word "miracle" from an essay by poet June Jordan, "The Difficult Miracle of Black Poetry in America, or Something Like a Sonnet for Phillis Wheatley" (2006). In her speech "The Transformation of Silence into Language and Action," (1977) Audre Lorde said: "For to survive in the mouth of this dragon we call america, we have had to learn this first and most vital lesson—that we were never meant to survive. Not as human beings." "Still we rise" is a hat-tip to Maya Angelou's beloved poem "And Still I Rise." I was thinking specifically of professional athletes Serena Williams and Simone Biles, as well as the Black women of NASA featured in the 2017 film *Hidden Figures*: Katherine Johnson, Dorothy Vaughan, and Mary Jackson.

"Lullaby"

This poem references the murder of several Black youth: In 2014 twelve-year-old Tamir Rice was shot and killed by a Cleveland police officer while playing in a park with a toy gun; in 2015 fifteen-year-old Dajerria Becton was brutalized by a police officer in McKinney, Texas, while attending a pool party; in 2015 sixteen-year-old Shakara was dragged from her desk and thrown to the floor by a school officer in Columbia, South Carolina; in 2010 seven-year-old Aiyana Stanley-Jones was shot and killed by police as she slept on the sofa of her grandmother's living room in Detroit; in 2012 twenty-two-year-old Rekia Boyd was shot and killed by off-duty Chicago police detective Dante Servin; in 1991 fifteen-year-old Latasha Harlins was shot and killed by store owner Soon Ja Du after being falsely accused of stealing a bottle of orange juice; in 2012 seventeen-year-old Trayvon Martin was shot and killed by vigilante George Zimmerman while walking home from the store with a bag of candy and a bottle of fruit punch.

"Black Lives Matter"

This poem is a tribute to the three founders of the Black Lives Matter movement: Alicia Garza, Opal Tometi, and Patrisse Khan-Cullors. The final words, "this steady love," are taken from Patrisse's 2018 memoir, *When They Call You a Terrorist.*

"Don't Touch My Hair"

Across the country and around the world Black girls have faced bullying and even suspension for the way they wear their hair. Black hair is political; we are judged by those outside our community, but we also judge one another sometimes. Learning to embrace and care for our hair is also political.

"Panther"

This poem blends references from the 2018 film *Black Panther* with the activism and values of the Black Panther Party. The Panthers were feared for their militant image and rhetoric, but beyond asserting Black people's Second Amendment right to bear arms, they ran a free breakfast program, operated health clinics, and taught Black children about their heritage. I also borrowed from Nina Simone's 1967 song "I Wish I Knew How It Would Feel to Be Free" (written by Billy Taylor and Dick Dallas).

Haiku 2

The danger of "driving while Black and woman" is a reference to Sandra Bland, who died in police custody after being pulled over in Texas for failing to signal a lane change.

"I question America" is taken from the testimony of Fannie Lou Hamer, an activist from Mississippi who was brutalized by police for demanding voting rights for African Americans. In 1964 she told of the abuse she endured and challenged the Credentials Committee at the Democratic National Convention.

The phrase "when the sea turns back" is from Audre Lorde's "A Woman Speaks."

"for my people"

I wrote this poem for anyone who's been shunned or shamed for not being "Black enough." I alluded to other outliers like Josephine Baker, who infamously strolled through Paris with a leopard named Chiquita on a leash. Riding on alligators refers to the lyrics of Beyoncé's song "Formation" from her 2016 album *Lemonade*.

"Sonnet for Ida"

Ida B. Wells, antilynching crusader and journalist, urged African Americans to migrate from the South to the Midwest. In her memoir, *Crusade for Justice*, Wells wrote: "if it were possible, [I] would gather my race in my arms and fly away with them."

"Mermaids"

The first line of this poem is taken from "A Woman Speaks" by Audre Lorde. I use her verse to address the migrant crisis in the Mediterranean, where, in 2017, twenty-six Nigerian teenage girls drowned. I also reference the kidnapping, rape, and forced marriage of Nigerian girls by Boko Haram, some of whom escaped and made their way home. I call their story "grim" as a way of evoking *Grimm's Fairy Tales*, full of magic and danger—for girls especially. In 1781 a British slave ship, the *Zong*, emptied its cargo of enslaved Africans into the sea in order to collect the insurance money. The "mother of the sea" I reference is Yemoja (also known as Yemaya in the Americas), a Yoruba orisha whose domain is the sea.

"tsunami"

This poem references acts of resistance taken by Colin Kaepernick, Bree Newsome, and Takiyah Thompson. NFL quarterback Kaepernick protested the police killing of unarmed Black people by kneeling during the national anthem; in 2015 Newsome climbed a thirty-foot pole to remove the Confederate flag from the South Carolina statehouse; Thompson, a student at North Carolina Central University, was arrested after toppling a Confederate monument on campus in 2017.

Haiku 3

Many Black women have claimed the title "queen" as a way to honor and uplift their sisters and themselves. I respect that choice. I grew up in a former British colony; at school each day I sang "God Save the Queen," and the image of Queen Elizabeth II was on Canadian currency. I am not a monarchist and feel the concept of queenhood—particularly when used by men—doesn't really serve women since it elevates one above all others (and not on the basis of merit). This haiku was inspired by this line from the Combahee River Collective's 1977 statement: "We reject pedestals, queenhood, and walking ten paces behind. To be recognized as human, levelly human, is enough."

The third haiku refers to the 2014 video of an altercation in an elevator between Solange Knowles and her sister Beyoncé's husband, Jay-Z.

"We Are Wise"

This poem and "We Can't Breathe" are inspired by Gwendolyn Brooks's 1959 poem "We Real Cool." In 2014 a police officer in Staten Island, NY, used an illegal chokehold to subdue and ultimately kill Eric Garner; Garner's last words were "I can't breathe."

"The Source"

Outrage around the 2018 murder of Stephon Clark by Sacramento police was complicated by colorist tweets he is alleged to have made three years prior to his death, including "I don't want nothin black but a Xbox." Some Black women felt ambivalent about and/or betrayed by Clark's remarks and refused to protest his death at the hands of police.

"Sacred"

I was raised in a devout Christian family; I am not religious now, but I can still recite one passage from the Bible: 1 Corinthians 6:19–20. Here's how it sounds in my head, at least: "Do you not know that your body is a temple of the Holy Spirit within you, which you have from God? You are not your own; you were bought with a price. So glorify God in your body."

With this poem I wanted to contrast the messages young women receive ("to be valued you must be perfect/pure") with the relative silence around the behavior and attitudes of young men who too often see Black girls as anything but sacred.

"Say Her Name"

The last stanza of this rondeau paraphrases a quote by James Baldwin. In "As Much Truth As One Can Bear," published in 1962 in the *New York Times Book Review*, Baldwin wrote: "Not everything that is faced can be solved, but nothing can be changed until it is faced."

Haiku 4

I borrowed "starshine and clay" from Lucille Clifton's poem "won't you celebrate with me." Astrophysicists have proven that all matter on Earth and in the universe originates from the residue or dust of dying stars.

"To Be Free"

This villanelle takes its two refrains from Nina Simone's song "I Wish I Knew How It Would Feel to Be Free" (written by Billy Taylor and Dick Dallas) and Octavia Butler's 1993 novel *Parable of the Sower* ("The destiny of Earthseed is to take root among the stars").

"The Crown"

This poem critiques the patriarchal assumption that only men can or should lead. In response to the degradation Black people continue to endure within a White supremacist society, some reach for uplifting metaphors and/or titles that don't actually promote equality. We can't fight dominance by reproducing it in our communities, our families, and/or our personal relationships. To quote the Combahee River Collective once more: "To be recognized as human, levelly human, is enough."

"anansi"

In West African and Caribbean folklore, Anansi is a trickster figure who can be human but often takes the form of a spider. Anansi is known by other names, including Aunt Nancy, and so in this poem I appeal to her to share her legendary storytelling skills so that I, too, may ensnare listeners.

"runaway"

This poem explores the Black feminist model of leadership using imagery from a fugitive slave's flight to freedom. The final four lines evoke Fanny Lou Hamer's declaration from a 1971 speech, "Nobody's Free Until Everybody's Free."

"On Being Builders of a New World"

This poem was inspired by "On Being Brought from Africa to America" by Phillis Wheatley, an enslaved eighteenth-century teen poet and the first Black person to publish a book of poetry in the United States. The opening line is borrowed from Rev. Martin Luther King Jr., who said in a 1966 interview, "I think that we've got to see that a riot is the language of the unheard." The phrase "dreams deferred" is a reference to Langston Hughes's 1951 poem "Harlem."

"Ascension"

This poem was inspired by the brutal 2018 murder of fifteen-year-old Sabriya McLean. The teen was stabbed almost eighty times before her body was set on fire and buried beneath a pile of leaves. A young African American man she'd met online was arrested. The murder took place in my West Philadelphia neighborhood just a few days before Christmas; I was reading Nnedi Okorafor's *The Book of Phoenix* at the time and so imagined Sabriya regenerating and taking flight. The winter solstice coincided with a meteor shower and full moon (the Cold Moon), and so I imagined the spirits of murdered Black women streaking across the sky. Black women are more likely than all other women in the US to be victims of homicide. The final lines of the poem are in Latin from the song "Pie Jesu"—"Pious Jesus/ Give them rest."

"Free Them All"

Bresha Meadows was fourteen years old when she was charged with aggravated murder for shooting her abusive father; she was released from custody two years later in 2018. CeCe McDonald is a transgender woman who was imprisoned after killing a transphobic man in self-defense; housed in men's prisons, she was released in 2014. Ahed Tamimi is a Palestinian teenager who was arrested at age sixteen for slapping and kicking an Israeli soldier attempting to enter her home; she was released in 2018 after serving an eight-month sentence. At age sixteen, sex-trafficking victim Cyntoia Brown was convicted of first-degree murder and robbery; Tennessee law requires that she serve a minimum of 51 years in prison. Cyntoia received clemency from Governor Bill Haslam in 2019.

"Mouse"

This dramatic monologue was inspired by *Out in the Night*, a 2014 documentary about the New Jersey 4. In 2006 a group of seven Black lesbians was sexually harassed and attacked by a homophobic straight Black man in the Village in New York City; when they defended themselves, they were arrested and four refused to take a plea. The press dubbed them "killer lesbians" and a "wolf pack." The documentary interviews Renata Hill, Patreese Johnson, Venice Brown, and Terrain Dandridge as they fight the charges of gang assault and attempted murder while trying to keep their families together. Patreese was convicted and given the longest sentence because she used a small knife to defend Venice. Carrying a knife was suggested by her brothers; one was shot by police as a teen, and another died while she was imprisoned. This poem is a fictionalized account.

"Get Up"

This poem opens with lyrics from James Brown's 1970 song "Get Up (I Feel Like Being A) Sex Machine" (co-written by Bobby Byrd) and then shifts to lyrics from Nina Simone's 1965 song "You've Got to Learn" (written by Charles Aznavour and Marcel Stellman).

Haiku 6

"Inherent value" is taken from the Combahee River Collective's 1977 statement: "Above all else, Our politics initially sprang from the shared belief that Black women are inherently valuable, that our liberation is a necessity not as an adjunct to somebody else's may because of our need as human persons for autonomy."

"Men Made of Glass"

This poem speaks to the phenomenon called "male fragility" whereby men respond to challenges to their authority with violence. The warning "beware my smile" is borrowed from "A Woman Speaks" by Audre Lorde; "indefensible panic" refers to the sham defense used by straight cisgender men who murder transgender women.

"a big blue sky poem"

This poem was inspired by "For Saundra" by Nikki Giovanni. The reference to Sojourner Truth's mother comes from another poem, "Oriflamme" by Jessie Redmon Fauset, originally published in the January 1920 issue of *The Crisis*.

ACKNOWLEDGMENTS

I didn't discover the tradition of Black women writers until I was in my twenties. I could have named a few authors as a teen, but I had no idea that women of African descent were writing novels, poems, stories, and plays all around the world—and had been telling stories about our lives for generations. When you realize that your small, soft voice is actually part of a chorus, you begin to sing with more confidence. I am grateful for every educator, friend, and mentor who shared their favorite Black feminist authors and texts with me, and it's an honor to be able to share some of my favorite poems in this collection. I thank the literary executors of Lucille Clifton and Audre Lorde, and appreciate the generosity of Nikki Giovanni in allowing me to place her poem alongside my own. I would like to thank my friends Rosamond S. King and Kate Foster for looking at the manuscript in its early stages; I appreciate the feedback my nieces Maya and Portia gave me on the cover. Cynthia Manick's expert eye brought order to this collection, and I am grateful for her editorial advice. I thank Paquita Campoverde of the Brooklyn Public Library for giving me the chance to teach the poetry workshops that inspired many of these poems. I thank Loveis Wise for creating vibrant, dynamic illustrations that perfectly capture the magic of us. Jennifer Laughran successfully found a home for my work, and, despite some unexpected setbacks, the Disney team rallied to produce a beautiful book.

Before this collection is published, more lives will likely be lost. We will mourn, we will mobilize, and we will memorialize our sisters by continuing to say their names.

CREDITS

Zetta Elliott is an award-winning author, scholar, and activist. Born in Canada, she moved to the US in 1994 to pursue her PhD in American Studies at NYU. She taught Black Studies at the college level for close to a decade and has worked with urban youth for thirty years. Her poetry has been published in *New Daughters of Africa*; *We Rise, We Resist, We Raise Our Voices*; the Cave Canem anthology *The Ringing Ear: Black Poets Lean South*; *Check the Rhyme: An Anthology of Female Poets and Emcees*; and *Coloring Book: An Eclectic Anthology of Fiction and Poetry by Multicultural Writers*. She is the author of over thirty books for young readers and currently lives in Lancaster, Pennsylvania. Visit zettaelliott.com to learn more.

Loveis Wise is a freelance illustrator and designer from Washington, DC. Her work can be found in the *New York Times*, the *New Yorker*, Refinery29, and Buzzfeed. She currently lives in Philadelphia.